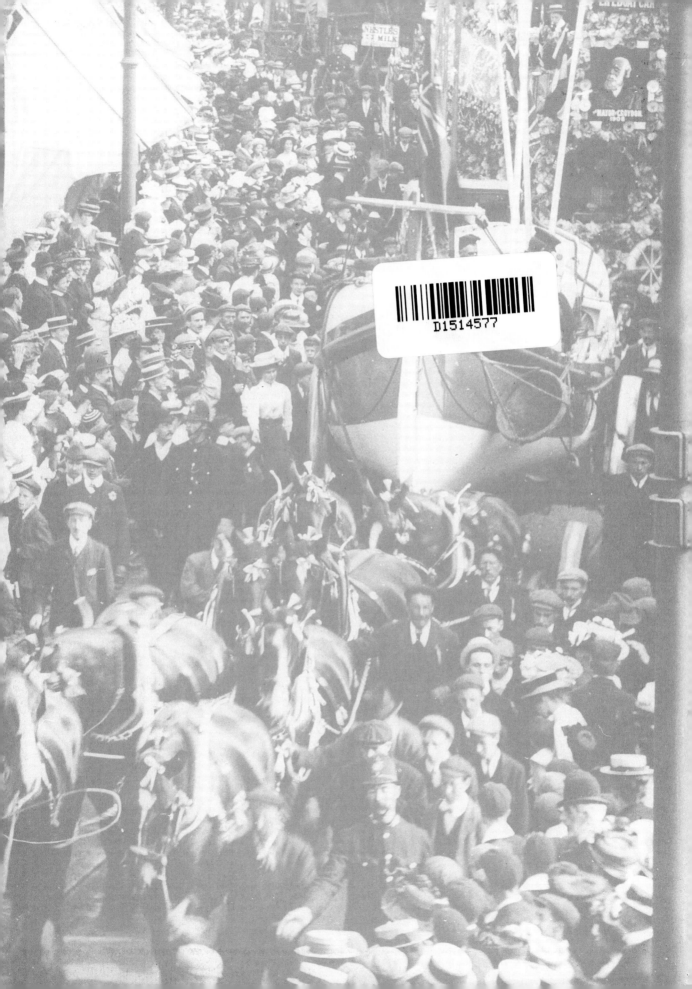

A CENTURY *of*
CROYDON

North End, 1995. The town's main shopping street from the late nineteenth century, it was pedestrianised in the 1980s and is usually thronged with shoppers. The Town Hall tower is a prominent landmark in the distance. (*John Gent*)

A CENTURY *of* CROYDON

JOHN GENT

SUTTON PUBLISHING

First published in the United Kingdom in 2000 by
Sutton Publishing Limited · Phoenix Mill
Thrupp · Stroud · Gloucestershire · GL5 2BU

British Library Cataloguing in Publication Data
A catalogue record for this book is available from the British Library.

ISBN 0-7509-2622-8

Front endpaper: Lifeboat Day, 1908. On Wednesday 20 July a great carnival was held to raise funds for the lifeboat service. There were two separate processions and this one, in High Street passing the corner of Surrey Street, included the Eastbourne lifeboat, drawn by eight horses. The other included the Southend lifeboat; the two processions joined at Broad Green. All the town's trams carried collecting boxes, and the tram in the background was illuminated and toured the town during the evening. ((*John Gent Collection*)

Back endpaper: Fair at Shirley Hills, 1938. The Addington Hills (generally known as Shirley Hills) have long attracted many visitors and day trippers, including Sunday School treats. This photograph shows the last fair to be held on the hills. (*Croydon Advertiser*)

Half title page: Samuel Coleridge Taylor. Croydon's most famous composer was born in London in 1875, but lived in the town from 1876 until his early death in 1912. He first conducted his own and other works at the Crystal Palace in 1898, and the composition for which he is best known, *The Song of Hiawatha*, at the Royal Albert Hall in 1900. He was very active in Croydon's musical life. (*John Gent Collection*)

Title page: Green Lane, Norbury, *c.* 1910. Two children enjoying the delights of this rural part of Croydon, still separating the town from the built-up mass of London. Houses would transform the scene in the early 1920s. (*John Gent Collection*)

 Published in association with 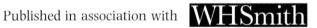 WHSmith

Typeset in 11/14pt Photina.
Typesetting and origination by
Sutton Publishing Limited.
Printed in Great Britain by
The Bath Press, Bath.

Dr Oscar Holden. Croydon's Medical Officer of Health inspects a Mobile Dressing Station at Mayday Hospital early in the war. (*Croydon Advertiser*)

Contents

The Whitgift Hospital, *c.* 1910. The most familiar landmark in the town centre linking the past and the present is the Whitgift Hospital, founded in 1596. It is still in use for its original purpose as almshouses and the quadrangle is a haven of peace and quiet in the heart of the town. (*John Gent Collection*)

Foreword

BY THE MAYOR OF CROYDON
COUNCILLOR MARY WALKER

In 1971 when I came to live in Croydon I knew very little about its history apart from Archbishop Whitgift and Croydon Airport. Thirty years on and I know a great deal more and I am fascinated by the history of our town.

In the past 100 years, Croydon has changed from a substantial market town surrounded by attractive countryside to one of the foremost business, retail and residential centres in the south-east of England.

Forestdale has replaced smallholdings, Park Hill's large Victorian houses have made way for well-planned flats and family houses and New Addington is now a small town where farms previously flourished.

Croydon Airport and its part in the history of aviation is remembered by the Amy Johnson and Jim Mollison Suites in the refurbished terminal building which now consists of a thriving office development housing almost 100 small and medium size companies.

It is estimated that 69,000 people commute from East Croydon station to London daily and a comparable number travel into the town to work in government, headquarters and other offices which dominate the skyline with their height and central location.

Fast north/south rail links with London, Gatwick and the south coast have been added to, with the reintroduction of trams. Tramlink operates three branch lines over 28 kilometres from east to west from Beckenham, New Addington and Wimbledon with a loop around the town centre putting Croydon once again in the forefront.

Croydon in 2000 is the largest London borough by population. Its people are racially and culturally diverse and all its residents have responded to rapidly changing times to make Croydon a town of continuing opportunity.

This book with its unique and fascinating collection of photographs traces the history of Croydon over the past 100 years and demonstrates the ever-changing face of a much loved town.

Mary Walker
Mayor

Fair at Shirley Hills, 1938. The Addington Hills (generally known as Shirley Hills) have long attracted many visitors and day trippers, including Sunday School treats. This photograph shows the last fair to be held on the hills. (*Croydon Advertiser*)

Britain: A Century of Change

Two women encumbered with gas masks go about their daily tasks during the early days of the war. (*Hulton Getty Picture Collection*)

The sixty years ending in 1900 were a period of huge trans-
formation for Britain. Railway stations, post-and-telegraph offices,
police and fire stations, gasworks and gasometers, new livestock
markets and covered markets, schools, churches, football grounds,
hospitals and asylums, water pumping stations and sewerage plants
totally altered the urban scene, and the country's population tripled with
more than seven out of ten people being born in or moving to the
towns. The century that followed, leading up to the Millennium's end in
2000, was to be a period of even greater change.

When Queen Victoria died in 1901, she was measured for her coffin
by her grandson Kaiser Wilhelm, the London prostitutes put on black
mourning and the blinds came down in the villas and terraces spreading
out from the old town centres. These centres were reachable by train
and tram, by the new bicycles and still newer motor cars, were connected by the new telephone, and lit by gas or even electricity. The shops
may have been full of British-made cotton and woollen clothing but the
grocers and butchers were selling cheap Danish bacon, Argentinian
beef, Australasian mutton and tinned or dried fish and fruit from
Canada, California and South Africa. Most of these goods were carried
in British-built-and-crewed ships burning Welsh steam coal.

As the first decade moved on, the Open Spaces Act meant more parks,
bowling greens and cricket pitches. The First World War transformed
the place of women, as they took over many men's jobs. Its other
legacies were the war memorials which joined the statues of Victorian
worthies in main squares round the land. After 1918 death duties and
higher taxation bit hard, and a quarter of England changed hands in
the space of only a few years.

The multiple shop – the chain store – appeared in the high street:
Sainsburys, Maypole, Lipton's, Home & Colonial, the Fifty Shilling Tailor,
Burton, Boots, W.H. Smith. The shopper was spoilt for choice, attracted
by the brash fascias and advertising hoardings for national brands like
Bovril, Pears Soap, and Ovaltine. Many new buildings began to be seen,
such as garages, motor showrooms, picture palaces (cinemas), 'palais de
dance', and ribbons of 'semis' stretched along the roads and new
bypasses and onto the new estates nudging the green belts.

During the 1920s cars became more reliable and sophisticated as well
as commonplace, with developments like the electric self-starter making
them easier for women to drive. Who wanted to turn a crank handle in
the new short skirt? This was, indeed, the electric age as much as the
motor era. Trolley buses, electric trams and trains extended mass
transport and electric light replaced gas in the street and the home,
which itself was groomed by the vacuum cleaner.

A major jolt to the march onward and upward was administered by
the Great Depression of the early 1930s. The older British industries –

textiles, shipbuilding, iron, steel, coal – were already under pressure from foreign competition when this worldwide slump arrived. Luckily there were new diversions to alleviate the misery. The 'talkies' arrived in the cinemas; more and more radios and gramophones were to be found in people's homes; there were new women's magazines, with fashion, cookery tips and problem pages; football pools; the flying feats of women pilots like Amy Johnson; the Loch Ness Monster; cheap chocolate and the drama of Edward VIII's abdication.

Things were looking up again by 1936 and new light industry was booming in the Home Counties as factories struggled to keep up with the demand for radios, radiograms, cars and electronic goods, including the first television sets. The threat from Hitler's Germany meant rearmament, particularly of the airforce, which stimulated aircraft and aero engine firms. If you were lucky and lived in the south, there was good money to be earned. A semi-detached house cost £450, a Morris Cowley £150. People may have smoked like chimneys but life expectancy, since 1918, was up by 15 years while the birth rate had almost halved.

In some ways it is the little memories that seem to linger longest from the Second World War: the kerbs painted white to show up in the

A W.H.Smith shop front in Beaconsfield, 1922.

blackout, the rattle of ack-ack shrapnel on roof tiles, sparrows killed by bomb blast. The biggest damage, apart from London, was in the south-west (Plymouth, Bristol) and the Midlands (Coventry, Birmingham). Postwar reconstruction was rooted in the Beveridge Report which set out the expectations for the Welfare State. This, together with the nationalisation of the Bank of England, coal, gas, electricity and the railways, formed the programme of the Labour government in 1945.

Children collecting aluminium to help the war effort, London, 1940s. (*IWM*)

Times were hard in the late 1940s, with rationing even more stringent than during the war. Yet this was, as has been said, 'an innocent and well-behaved era'. The first let-up came in 1951 with the Festival of Britain and there was another fillip in 1953 from the Coronation, which incidentally gave a huge boost to the spread of TV. By 1954 leisure motoring had been resumed but the Comet – Britain's best hope for taking on the American aviation industry – suffered a series of mysterious crashes. The Suez debacle of 1956 was followed by an acceleration in the withdrawal from Empire, which had begun in 1947 with the Independence of India. Consumerism was truly born with the advent of commercial TV and most homes soon boasted washing machines, fridges, electric irons and fires.

A street party to celebrate the Queen's Coronation, June 1953. (*Hulton Getty Picture Collection*)

The *Lady Chatterley* obscenity trial in 1960 was something of a straw in the wind for what was to follow in that decade. A collective loss of inhibition seemed to sweep the land, as the Beatles and the Rolling Stones transformed popular music, and retailing, cinema and the theatre were revolutionised. Designers, hair-dressers, photographers and models moved into places vacated by an Establishment put to flight by the new breed of satirists spawned by *Beyond the Fringe* and *Private Eye*.

In the 1970s Britain seems to have suffered a prolonged hangover after the excesses of the previous decade. Ulster, inflation and union troubles were not made up for by entry into the EEC, North Sea Oil, Women's Lib or, indeed, Punk Rock. Mrs Thatcher applied the corrective in the 1980s,

as the country moved more and more from its old manufacturing base over to providing services, consulting, advertising, and expertise in the 'invisible' market of high finance or in IT.

The post-1945 townscape has seen changes to match those in the worlds of work, entertainment and politics. In 1952 the Clean Air Act served notice on smogs and pea-souper fogs, smuts and blackened buildings, forcing people to stop burning coal and go over to smokeless sources of heat and energy. In the same decade some of the best urban building took place in the 'new towns' like Basildon, Crawley, Stevenage and Harlow. Elsewhere open warfare was declared on slums and what was labelled inadequate, cramped, back-to-back, two-up, two-down, housing. The new 'machine for living in' was a flat in a high-rise block. The architects and planners who promoted these were in league with the traffic engineers, determined to keep the motor car moving whatever the price in multi-storey car parks, meters, traffic wardens and ring roads. The old pollutant, coal smoke, was replaced by petrol and diesel exhaust, and traffic noise.

Fast food was no longer only a pork pie in a pub or fish-and-chips. There were Indian curry houses, Chinese take-aways and American-style hamburgers, while the drinker could get away from beer in a wine bar. Under the impact of television

Punk rockers demonstrate their anarchic style during the 1970s. (*Barnaby's Picture Library*)

the big Gaumonts and Odeons closed or were rebuilt as multi-screen cinemas, while the palais de dance gave way to discos and clubs.

From the late 1960s the introduction of listed buildings and conservation areas, together with the growth of preservation societies, put a brake on 'comprehensive redevelopment'. The end of the century and the start of the Third Millennium see new challenges to the health of towns and the wellbeing of the nine out of ten people who now live urban lives. The fight is on to prevent town centres from dying, as patterns of housing and shopping change, and edge-of-town supermarkets exercise the attractions of one-stop shopping. But as banks and department stores close, following the haberdashers, greengrocers, butchers and ironmongers, there are signs of new growth such as farmers' markets, and corner stores acting as pick-up points where customers collect shopping ordered on-line from web sites.

Futurologists tell us that we are in stage two of the consumer revolution: a shift from mass consumption to mass customisation driven by a

Millennium celebrations over the Thames
at Westminster, New Year's Eve, 1999.
(*Barnaby's Picture Library*)

desire to have things that fit us and our particular lifestyle exactly, and
for better service. This must offer hope for small city-centre shop
premises, as must the continued attraction of physical shopping,
browsing and being part of a crowd: in a word, 'shoppertainment'.
Another hopeful trend for towns is the growth in the number of young
people postponing marriage and looking to live independently, alone,
where there is a buzz, in 'swinging single cities'. Their's is a 'flats-and-
cafés' lifestyle, in contrast to the 'family suburbs', and certainly fits in
with government's aim of building 60 per cent of the huge amount of
new housing needed on 'brown' sites, recycled urban land. There looks
to be plenty of life in the British town yet.

Croydon: An Introduction

During the nineteenth century Croydon grew from a small but important market town with a population of just under 6,000 to a flourishing county borough with a population of more than 130,000. At the beginning of the twentieth century the borough boundaries mostly coincided with those of the ancient parish and had remained virtually unchanged for nearly 1,000 years. They included the growing districts of Upper and South Norwood, Norbury, Thornton Heath, Selhurst, Addiscombe, Woodside, Shirley, Waddon and part of Purley to the south. To the north the wooded heights of Norwood, and areas of farmland around Norbury, still maintained a break from the engulfing spread of both London and Croydon. Southwards the rolling hills and valleys of the North Downs were still largely open and in places the landscape was similar to parts of the South Downs today.

In 1900 Addington, Sanderstead and Coulsdon with their medieval churches were remote rural communities, the combined population of

Croydon Palace, 1999. The view of the Palace from the tower of the Parish Church shows that much of this lovely old building survives. It was Croydon's original manor house and was for centuries used by the Archbishops of Canterbury as their near London, country residence. They ceased to use it in the mid-eighteenth century and it became a factory, and later a school. At one time it was surrounded by extensive grounds and streams which formed one of the sources of the River Wandle. It is now the home of the Old Palace School of John Whitgift. (*John Gent*)

Croydon town centre, 1964. The large-scale redevelopment of the central area started in 1959 and was well under way five years later. The Trinity School playing fields were still a green oasis but would soon become a building site for the Whitgift Shopping Centre. St George's House is on the left, and Fairfield on the right. The car park between the Fairfield Halls and the Technical College was not yet covered in, and construction of the Park Lane Underpass was in progress. (*Chorley Handford*)

the three parishes totalling only 8,000. They were part of a large area administered by the Croydon Rural District Council, which also included Merton, Morden and Mitcham. In 1915 the Rural District Council was abolished and Coulsdon and Purley Urban District Council was formed to include Coulsdon, most of Purley, Kenley, Selsdon and Sanderstead. Addington remained separate until 1928 when it became part of Croydon. In 1965 the Coulsdon and Purley area was amalgamated with Croydon to form one of the new London boroughs, with a population of around 330,000.

This book attempts to give some photographic coverage of the whole of the present London borough, so that all parts are represented. However, the majority of the photographs are of Croydon itself because it is the natural centre for the area around it and is where many local people have traditionally worked, shopped and spent much of their leisure time. The pictures include numerous events and civic occasions, and show many ordinary townspeople as they went about their daily lives.

Throughout the twentieth century building development continued, with wartime interruptions, as the farms, woods and downland were gradually covered by new houses. Large homes in spacious grounds were slowly surrounded by small houses as part of their land was sold off and, in many cases, they too eventually succumbed to the developer.

From the 1960s, many of the larger Victorian houses, often on 99-year leases, had become too large for modern needs and, particularly in areas such as Upper Norwood, Park Hill and Kenley, have been replaced by blocks of flats or new 'executive' homes.

By the 1920s, motor traffic was increasing and the narrow streets in the town centre were becoming very congested. Purley Way was built as one of the first by-passes in the country, opening in 1924/5. New terminal buildings for Croydon Airport opened in 1928 with a frontage on to the new road. Soon the area attracted a great deal of industrial development, mainly light engineering. By the middle of the century Croydon had a wide variety of manufacturing activities here in addition to many already existing in other parts of the town. Companies such as Trojan Motors, Powers Samas, Philips, Fords, Creeds, Bourjois and Mullards had local factories. By the 1970s there were over 1,000 factories and workshops in the borough. Many were quite small but there was employment for over 28,000 people in engineering alone. Unfortunately, the general decline in light industry throughout the country has led to major changes in Croydon too. Purley Way now has a wide range of large warehouse-type stores including IKEA, much less industry, much less employment, and much greater traffic problems! The by-pass itself now needs a by-pass.

Two wars left their mark on the town which received one serious air attack in the First World War and many in the Second. In 1940, as the Battle of Britain raged in the skies above, fighter aircraft from Croydon played an important part in the conflict together with those from Kenley and Biggin Hill only a few miles to the south.

In the 1950s, Croydon Council obtained approval for its ambitious development plan and set aside 45 acres in the central area for major commercial development. The first new office block, Norfolk House, was let in 1959 and within ten years the skyline of the town had been transformed by the construction of forty-five such blocks. Inevitably, this led to the loss of some familiar landmarks and a total trans-formation of parts of the town centre. Further new schemes in the 1980s added more office space and the town is now the sixth largest commercial centre in the country.

Croydon is often maligned, mainly by those who know nothing of it apart from the tower blocks that give it the image of a mini-Manhattan. A few years ago a journalist wrote that Croydon does not fit in with the image of neat surburbia and therefore is a conceptual anachronism with the feel of a Midlands manufacturing town in the midst of dormitory suburbs. This is because it has grown over a long period with its own suburbs growing out to meet those of London, and eventually being engulfed. Factories, churches, schools, parks, woods, golf courses, allotments, offices, local shopping centres and a great variety of types of housing all mixed up with its hilly terrain combine to form its essential character as a provincial town within the mass of London.

As a county borough, Croydon was largely independent until the 1930s, with its own tramways, electricity and water undertakings, fire brigade, ambulance service and hospitals. Motor vehicles registered here carried local letters – BY, VB, RK and OY. Hall and Company, with branches throughout the south-east, and many other smaller firms, carried the name of the town on their vehicles. Now large national combines have replaced most of these smaller companies.

The nature of the population has changed too. There is generally less stability with the widespread loss of 'jobs

Happy Valley from Farthing Downs, Coulsdon, 1995. Building development covered many parts of the downs to the south of Croydon during the twentieth century. However, some areas such as this, Kenley Common and Riddlesdown, have been preserved as public open spaces. They provide excellent opportunities for very attractive country walks. (*John Gent*)

for life' while the motor car is seen by many as giving the freedom to live and work in places far apart. Many people have moved into the area from countries far away and are now Croydonians. They have been largely welcomed, but the ethnic diversity now apparent sometimes causes a few minor problems. There are parts of the borough that suffer a degree of social deprivation but the town enters the twenty-first century with good prospects. Major redevelopment schemes are planned and it is to be hoped they will all materialise. These include a large arena, hotel, retail and commercial scheme for the former railway goods yard at East Croydon; Croydon Centrale as an extension of the Drummond Centre; Park Place on the site of St George's Walk; and the Grant's entertainment and leisure complex which is currently under construction. The Skyline Project is an imaginative lighting scheme for illuminating many of the office blocks at night. Tramlink provides excellent east–west links that should, with the good rail connections already in place, allow for a reduction in traffic levels. There is every sign that Croydon will maintain its position as a significant regional business, shopping and leisure centre. With a wide variety of good housing and schools, excellent transport links, splendid parks and open spaces, the foundations laid by Croydonians in the twenieth century should last well into the future for the city within a city.

Before the Great Conflict

The Grand Theatre and Opera House, Croydon High Street, *c.* 1906. Opened in 1896, the theatre had a splendidly ornate late Victorian interior and was a much-loved local venue. Declining attendances forced its closure and demolition in 1959 despite determined local efforts to save it for the town. The site is now occupied by an office block, Grosvenor House. (*John Gent Collection*)

Croydon horse tram, *c.* 1900. It was decorated to celebrate either the Relief of Mafeking or the end of the Boer War. Horse trams were introduced by the Croydon Tramways Company in 1879. The system was bought by Croydon Corporation, reconstructed and replaced by electric trams in 1901/2. (*Croydon Public Libraries*)

Churchill Road, South Croydon, *c.* 1910. The road was built in the mid-1890s, while St Augustine's Church had opened to serve a growing district in 1883. A group of local children have gathered for the photographer. Perhaps one or two of them still live in the area. (*John Gent Collection*)

Woodside Sports, 1907. Woodside, with its green, still has much of the atmosphere of the village it was in earlier days. Some of the residents seem to have had lots of fun dressing up for the village sports over 90 years ago. (*John Gent Collection*)

Croham Hurst, *c.* 1908. This is a popular wooded hill in South Croydon with spectacular views. A threat to build houses on it at the end of the nineteenth century attracted much local opposition and eventually it was saved for the town. The fields in the distance were covered with houses by the mid-twentieth century. (*John Gent Collection*)

Harvesting, *c.* 1907. Much of Croydon was still farmland in the early years of the twentieth century. Children sometimes played truant to help with the harvest. Agricultural methods had changed little for centuries. Left to right

are J. Canfield, D. Doulton, A. Doulton, W. Richards and G. Leach. The children in front are G. Doulton and K. Doulton. The photograph is thought to have been taken at Waddon Court Farm. (*Croydon Public Libraries*)

Norbury Tram Terminus, *c.* 1910. The Corporation Tramways arrived here at the northern end of the borough in 1901 and from 1909 the London County Council Tramways were extended to meet them. It was not until 1926 that the tracks were joined and you could ride on a through tram from Croydon to London. (*John Gent Collection*)

Purley High Street, *c.* 1906. At the southern extremity of the old borough, the area developed as a popular residential district from the 1880s. Electric trams arrived in 1901 and the Brighton Road area, off the picture to the right, soon grew into a rather more important local shopping centre. (*John Gent Collection*)

Elgin Road, Addiscombe, *c.* 1910. It was built in the 1860s on part of the site of Addiscombe College, a military training establishment for the East India Company, which closed in 1859. Some of the houses were large, and the road is typical of many in Croydon where there is great variety of architectural styles because just a few houses were built at any one time, often by different small local builders. (*John Gent Collection*)

Macclesfield Road, South Norwood, *c.* 1910. This road was developed from 1905 and demonstrates smaller houses, again with several differing styles, and complete with a corner shop. Many similar shops existed until the 1960s but some have closed as supermarkets and out-of-town shopping centres have attracted most of the custom. (*John Gent Collection*)

The Croydon Ice Company's cart in Spa Road (now Northwood Road), 1905. It was not until after the Second World War that refrigerators became common. Before that ice had to be purchased from local suppliers. Most households kept meat and milk cool in hot weather by simple methods such as putting milk bottles in a bowl of cold water in a cool place and draping a cloth over them. (*John Gent Collection*)

Madam Florence, 17 June 1903. The Brighton Road has been, and still is from time to time, the scene of somewhat unusual, even eccentric events. Here Madam Florence, the American Globe Walker, is on her way from London to Brighton and passing Smitham Bottom, now the shopping centre of Coulsdon. (*John Gent Collection*)

Milk delivery cart at Duppas Hill. Such vehicles were common until the Second World War. The milk would be ladled out of the large churn into small containers – not a very hygienic method. (*John Gent Collection*)

Meet of Hounds at Addington, *c.* 1910. Croydon was a popular centre for fox-hunting in the early nineteenth century, with Londoners flocking to the town for the sport. As the town grew and the surrounding country was developed for housing, so the hunts moved further afield. (*Croydon Public Libraries*)

Cattle Market, *c.* 1909. For centuries Croydon was an important market town. In 1848 a purpose-built cattle market was provided on the southern edge of the town near the Swan and Sugar Loaf Hotel. Even as late as the 1920s a special weekly train from Tonbridge brought cattle in from Kent to the market but as the surrounding countryside was built over, the market declined, and it closed in 1935. Drovers Road is on the site. (*Croydon Public Libraries*)

The Wellington public house, *c.* 1910. A party is about to set off by horse-drawn wagon from the pub on the corner of Mitcham Road and Sumner Road. The outing was obviously going to be accompanied by music, and probably a certain amount of beer. The public house still exists but has recently been renamed the New Inn. (*John Gent Collection*)

The Public Halls looking east along George Street, *c.* 1910. Wellesley Road is on the left and Park Lane on the right. The Croydon Literary and Scientific Institution was formed in 1838 and built the Public Halls in 1860. Until the Second World War the halls were the venue for many theatrical and musical events, and for exhibitions. By then in the ownership of Croydon Council, they were little used afterwards as the Corporation had bought the North End Hall, which it ran as the Civic Hall from about 1940. The Public Halls were demolished in the late 1950s. Norfolk House and the underpass now occupy the site. The clock tower in the distance was part of Thrift's Grocery Warehouse, also demolished in the late 1950s. (*John Gent Collection*)

Inauguration of the Stanley Memorial Clocktower, South Norwood, June 1907. William Ford Stanley lived at Cumberlow, South Norwood, for over 40 years. He designed and built the Stanley Halls and Art Gallery on South Norwood Hill and later provided the Stanley Technical Trade School alongside – a prototype secondary technical school. The Clocktower at Station Road was provided by the residents of the area to celebrate Mr and Mrs Stanley's Golden Wedding. (*John Gent Collection*)

The Hippodrome on Crown Hill. Opened in 1910 on the site of the old Theatre Royal, initially it was a music hall with some film shows, but by 1918 it went over to showing films only. In 1929 it was the first London-area cinema outside the West End to show talking pictures. It closed in 1956 and was demolished. (*John Gent Collection*)

Covered Market, *c.* 1908. Built around 1906 in Elis David Place on the corner of Pitlake and Lower Church Street, it was used for fruit, vegetables and fish, but seems to have been unsuccessful. From about 1909 it became a cinema, The Dome. Later renamed The Olympia, it closed in 1916 and was used by Reeves as a furniture showroom until demolition for road improvements in 1973. (*John Gent Collection*)

Miss Kitty Oliver's class at Boston Road Board School, Thornton Heath, 1907. (*John Gent Collection*)

St Peter's Church United Football Club, 1913. Many churches and commercial organisations had teams which participated in a variety of sports. The team are seen displaying the cup of the Croydon and District Church League, which they had just won. (*John Gent Collection*)

The Croydon Temperance Silver Band, *c.* 1912. The temperance movement had a very strong following in the late Victorian and Edwardian periods. There were also many brass bands in most towns, and Croydon was no exception. The band appears to have won a shield and certificate, possibly at one of the brass band festivals at Crystal Palace. (*John Gent Collection*)

J.E. Killick's shop, *c.* 1914. The name of Killick is still a familiar one locally. This tobacconist's, confectioner's and newsagent's shop was at 190 Brighton Road, South Croydon, from about 1914 until the mid-1970s and changed very little in over 50 years. Presumably Toby, who ran it in later years, was one of the three children. (*John Gent Collection*)

Riddlesdown Tea Gardens, *c.* 1907. The downs to the south of Croydon were popular venues for outings and Sunday School Treats. In 1893 William Gardner opened a Pleasure Resort, Temperance Hotel and Tea Gardens at Riddlesdown. Attractions over the years included donkeys, a museum, monkey house, aviary, swings, hoop-la and a miniature railway. By 1906 refreshments could be provided for over 2,000 people at one time. William Gardner died in 1930 and part of the site was sold for development. (*John Gent Collection*)

The 1st Thornton Heath BP Scouts, *c.* 1914. The Boy Scout movement was founded in 1908 by Robert Baden-Powell. The BP Scouts was a breakaway section of the movement. (*John Gent Collection*)

Baker's handcart, c. 1910. Small handcarts like this were used extensively by bakers in the days when most tradesmen would deliver direct to your home. F.J. Hobden's shop was at 63 Tamworth Road on the opposite corner of Tamworth Place to the Tamworth Arms public house. (*John Gent Collection*)

Coach building, c. 1914. Abner Creasey established a coach-building business in Clifford Road, South Norwood, in 1888. By 1913 his business had moved to Pembury Road and this illustration shows work at his new premises. (*John Gent Collection*)

Mobilisation of Croydon Territorials, 5 August 1914. The 4th Queen's Royal West Surrey Regiment are here marching out of the barracks into Mitcham Road on the way to East Croydon station, whence they travelled to Strood by train. The barracks was established in 1794 and the original building can be seen in the right background. It was demolished in the 1950s but there are still barracks on the site. (*John Gent Collection*)

Recruiting in 1915. This empty shop was used for publicity purposes for a nearby recruiting office, thought to be at 42 London Road. (*Croydon Public Libraries*)

The First World War

Military parade, *c.* 1915. Troops marching along Croydon High Street, possibly part of the great recruiting procession that took place on 18 June 1915 when over 2,300 troops, with bands, marched through the town. The stencil 'TH' on the headlight of the tram denotes the destination 'Thornton Heath' to assist passengers in identifying their tram during the blackout. (*John Gent Collection*)

Bomb damage, 1915. There were numerous warnings of Zeppelin attacks on the area during the war, but there were few serious incidents locally. However, eighteen bombs were dropped on the town on 13 October 1915 and the damage caused by one that fell in Beech House Road is evident in this photograph. Three boys were killed but their father and the housekeeper survived. In the same raid, bombs fell in Chatsworth, Oval, Morland, Howard and Stretton Roads. In total 11 people were killed, 17 injured and damage was caused to about 800 buildings. (*Croydon Public Libraries*)

Red Cross procession, 1916. Croydon's Red Cross Week started on Saturday 22 January and the inaugural procession is passing through Katharine Street, watched by large crowds. The mayor, Alderman Frank Denning, later addressed the crowds from the steps of the Town Hall. The Kings Arms Hotel was one of the town's principal hotels but closed and was demolished when the St George's Walk development took place in the 1960s. (*John Gent Collection*)

Recruiting procession. On 2 October 1915, a great mile-long procession passed through the town to stimulate recruitment under the Derby Scheme. Some 2,800 soldiers and sailors were escorted by ten bands and the procession, here marching from St James's Road into London Road at Broad Green, finished at the Town Hall. The mayor, Alderman Frank Denning, and Captain Sir Edward Clark KC made speeches. The latter concluding by saying 'the man who serves his country now, will have the right to speak with pride to his son hereafter'. He might well have added 'if he survives'! Some 10,000 men were recruited voluntarily, largely as a result of this event. (*John Gent Collection*)

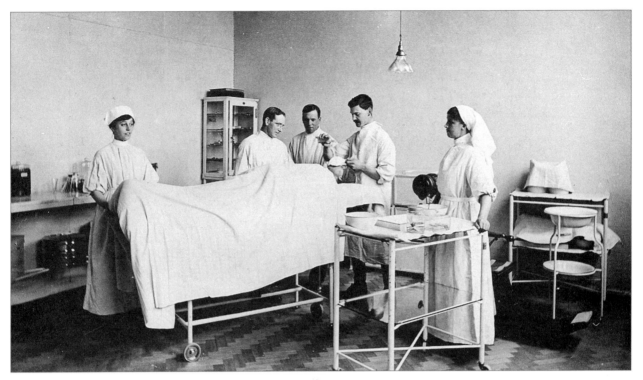

Operating Theatre, May 1918. Six council schools in Croydon were converted into War Hospitals, with 1,000 beds. The children from the closed schools were redistributed to others. The operating theatre at Stanford Road War Hospital in Norbury seems rather basic by modern standards. (*John Gent Collection*)

Dispensary, *c.* 1918. A nurse waits for some medicinal supplies to be made up at Stanford Road War Hospital. (*John Gent Collection*)

Kitchen, July 1917. Stanford Road War Hospital's kitchen was in a temporary building. The other war hospitals were at The Crescent, Davidson Road, Ingram Road and Ecclesbourne Road. Addington Palace was also used. (*John Gent Collection*)

Dining room, Ingram Road War Hospital. The school hall was used here as a dining room for the patients and while some appear fairly cheerful, others look far from happy – hardly surprising considering the awful time they must have been through. There were few amenities when the War Hospitals first opened and a War Hospitals Comforts Fund was set up. Many local people gave voluntary help, including Mrs Edgelow who served for three and a half years as the 'lady barber' at the Crescent Hospitals and in that time performed 42,000 haircuts as well as helping to shave patients in preparation for operations! (*John Gent Collection*)

North Surrey Golf Course, *c.* 1917. Patients from a local War Hospital were entertained to tea at the North Surrey Golf Course in Norbury. Fortunately the weather was kind. This golf course closed around 1935 and was purchased by Croydon Corporation: it is now Norbury Park. Golf is a popular sport locally and there are a number of courses in Croydon, many of them having been in existence from the early twentieth century. (*John Gent Collection*)

Tug-of-war, *c.* 1917. Patients from local War Hospitals are here being entertained at the Croydon Gas Company's sports ground at Waddon. Tug-of-war seems a somewhat surprising choice as an activity for wounded soldiers! (*John Gent Collection*)

Belgian School, *c.* 1916. In August 1914, the mayor, Alderman Frank Denning, opened a fund for the benefit of the Belgian refugees who were arriving in the town. Between 800 and 900 came in the early months of the war, including over 200 children under the age of sixteen. Belgian refugee nuns looked after some of these and this school was established in a private house somewhere in the town. Its location is not known. (*John Gent Collection*)

Sugar queue, 1917. Severe food shortages developed late in the war and Croydon Food Control Committee was set up in 1917. Sugar control started in September that year and this queue was photographed in Whitehorse Road. Other commodities such as meat and tea also became very scarce. General rationing was introduced in February 1918. (*John Gent Collection*)

London Road, Norbury. For most of the war, life at home went on much as normal. The street was very quiet at 8.00 a.m. on 1 April 1917 after an overnight showfall. No hardy souls seem to have been prepared to enjoy the delights of travelling on the open top of a Corporation tramcar. (*Croydon Public Libraries*)

Whitgift Founder's Day, 1918. Archbishop John Whitgift loved Croydon and on his death in 1604 he was buried in Croydon Parish Church. He founded a grammar school which eventually developed into the separate grammar and middle schools. Here the pupils of the Middle School, then situated in Church Road, prepare to march to the Parish Church for the annual Founder's Day Service. (*John Gent Collection*)

Firemen, 1916. Croydon Fire Brigade was mobilised on sixty-eight occasions during the war because of possible air raids. Chief Officer John Dane (centre) is accompanied by some members of the brigade, the fire station cat and, presumably, the brigade mascot – a budding young fireman. (*John Gent Collection*)

Women's Citizen's Day, 20 March 1918. Women had to fight hard for equal rights through most of the twentieth century. This day was a celebration of franchise reform. Many Croydonians had been active in the suffrage movement and a procession of women marched to the Town Hall where the mayoress, Mrs Houlder, presented an address to her husband, the mayor, Alderman Howard Houlder. On the right is the Town Clerk, Dr John Newnham. Alderman Houlder was mayor in four successive years and both he and his wife were made Freemen of the town in 1920. (*John Gent Collection*)

National Aircraft Factory No. 1, 1918. This was built on 240 acres of land at Waddon to the west of Coldharbour Lane and south of Stafford Road. It included a flying testing ground, later to be known as Waddon Aerodrome. Production started in January 1918 but the war was over by November that year and work on aircraft ceased. In 1920 the factory was sold to Handley Page's Aircraft Disposal Company. The fuselage and jig-making shop is shown here. (*John Gent Collection*)

Peace Day, Saturday 19 July 1919. More than 2,500 Croydonians had been killed and many more injured by the end of the war. Peace Day was a national festival. Thousands of people thronged the streets to see the procession of service and ex-service men and women and local bands. This photograph was taken in Katharine Street outside the Town Hall as a Royal Naval contingent passed. There was dancing in the streets with bonfires and firework displays after dark. (*John Gent Collection*)

Briton Hill Farm, *c.* 1922. The relentless spread of suburbia continued between the wars. This view at Sanderstead shows new housing gradually spreading on to the downs south of Croydon, intermingled with farmland. Haystacks and stooks of corn were common until after the Second World. (*John Gent Collection*)

Shirley Way, *c.* 1933. Shirley was still fairly remote until the late 1920s/early 1930s when a great deal of housing development took place. There were no cars parked in the street at this time, and the young child on the tricycle could safely be allowed out in the street unsupervised. (*John Gent Collection*)

Between the Wars

Waddon Aerodrome post office, *c.* 1920. The aerodrome was known as Waddon for only a few years and the post office was very basic. Rohan et Cie operated a bookstall and provided postal facilities later in the new terminal buildings on Purley Way. (*John Gent Collection*)

Girl Guides, 1921. The movement was started by Robert Baden-Powell, his sister Agnes, and his wife Olave in 1910, two years after the Boy Scouts. Here a group of Girl Guides pose for a photograph on Croham Hurst in 1921. (*John Gent Collection*)

West & Hiscock's Family Butcher's shop, at 27 High Street, Thornton Heath, *c.* 1924. It was common for meat to be hung up outside the shops at this time but the practice was not very hygienic. (*John Gent Collection*)

Croydon General Hospital, 1926. The children's ward was decorated for Christmas, and the mayor, Councillor A.J. Camden Field, is paying a visit. Standing just in front of him is Lady Edridge and to the right of the tree is Alderman W.B. Southwell, mayor for the previous two years. It is to be hoped that Father Christmas did not set his beard on fire. (*John Gent Collection*)

Wandle Park, *c.* 1924. Opened in 1890 with a boating lake fed by the River Wandle which flowed through the land, it was very popular with Croydonians until the 1930s. However, the water supply became erratic and the lake often dried up. Eventually it was filled in and the river was put into a culvert in the late 1960s. (*John Gent Collection*)

Charabanc outing, early 1920s. A group is about to set off from the Sheldon Arms public house in Sheldon Street. Nobody is without a hat and most of the people are wearing a small flower but it is not known what this represented. The Sheldon Arms was demolished for the construction of the Old Town flyover in the 1960s. (*John Gent Collection*)

Croydon Airport, *c.* 1921. Beddington and Waddon Airfields opened in 1916 as part of the air defence of London. After the war it was decided to use them as the civil and customs airport for London and the combined fields opened as Croydon Airport in 1920. The original terminal building and control tower seen here were to the east of Plough Lane, but not within the Borough of Croydon. The airport at that time has been described as 'resembling a wild-west township in early mining days'. (*John Gent Collection*)

Aircraft interior, *c.* 1924. Early civil aircraft were very small by modern standards and could carry only a few passengers. This is an Imperial Airways' aircraft passenger saloon in the mid-1920s. (*John Gent Collection*)

Croydon Aerodrome Hotel, *c.* 1936. In 1928 a completely new terminal building and a hotel were built on the recently opened Purley Way to the east of the airfield. Many of the great events in civil aviation history took place at Croydon, and here large crowds have gathered on and around the Aerodrome Hotel to see the famous Amy Johnson arrive after one of her record-breaking flights. (*John Gent Collection*)

Croydon Airport, *c.* 1932. Horatius, one of the famous Handley Page HP 42 aircraft, flies over the control tower and terminal buildings in the early 1930s. The airport was taken over by the Royal Air Force at the outbreak of the Second World War and returned to civil use in 1946. However, it was too small for modern aircraft and it closed and was replaced by Gatwick in 1959. (*John Gent Collection*)

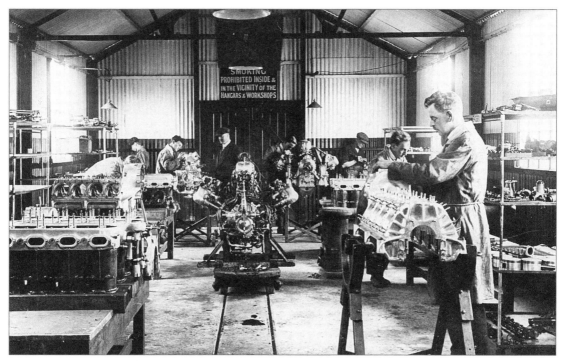

Aircraft engines being overhauled at Croydon Airport, *c.* 1930. (*John Gent Collection*)

Leathwood's Garages, *c.* 1927. Motor cars had gradually come into use from the last few years of the nineteenth century. By the 1920s they were much more common and Leathwood's Garages were a familiar part of the local scene. This rally of motor cars and motor cycles on their St James's Road forecourt includes a couple of Morgan three-wheelers and a Fraser Nash. (*John Gent Collection*)

Thornton Heath Station, *c.* 1925. Croydon became a popular residential area for commuters by the mid-nineteenth century and it was the railway that caused its rapid development from that time onwards. Here passengers are waiting on Thornton Heath station platform for the 8.10 a.m. train to Victoria. The gantry is for the overhead wires which were used by the London Brighton and South Coast Railway in the early electrification of some local lines from 1912 to 1925. Following the formation of the Southern Railway in 1923 it was decided to standardise on the third-rail system now in use, and the overhead masts and gantries at Thornton Heath were used for only three years. (*John Gent Collection*)

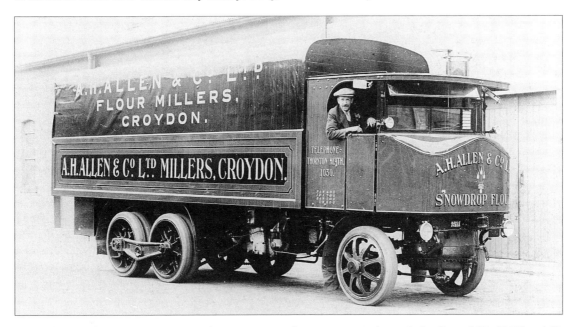

Sentinel steam lorry, *c.* 1925. Steam lorries were used quite extensively until the Second World War. A.H. Allen & Co. Ltd had their flour mill in St James's Road near Spurgeon's Bridge until the 1960s. The Wonderloaf Bakery was built on the site but has now been replaced by housing. As large companies take over smaller ones and rationalise their activities on to large sites there is a growing trend for local jobs to be lost and for small industrial buildings to be replaced by flats and houses. (*John Gent Collection*)

Bell Foundry, *c*. 1925. The clockmaking company became Gillett and Johnston in 1877, having been formed as Gillett and Bland in 1844. The firm added bell-founding to their activities and became famous during the first half of the twentieth century, sending their products to many parts of the world. Here a crowd of visitors is watching a bell being cast at the Whitehorse Road foundry in the 1920s. The firm closed the factory in the mid-1950s but their work continues on a more modest scale dealing only with clocks. (*John Gent Collection*)

North End, *c.* 1923. Looking towards West Croydon, the Empire Theatre is on the right. Opened in 1906, it was reconstructed from the former National Palace of Varieties and became the Eros cinema in 1953, before closure and demolition in 1959. The teashops of J. Lyons & Co. were common in most towns from late Edwardian days until the 1960s. There were three in Croydon town centre. (*John Gent Collection*)

Kenley, 1927. Boxing Day blizzards in December 1927 caused chaos in much of the south-east. Villages such as Chaldon, Tatsfield, Farleigh and Chelsham on the downs a few miles south of Croydon were cut off for nearly a week. By 31 December the BBC was broadcasting appeals for people to lay out black clothes to cover an area not less than 15 feet in diameter in the snow, to help pilots pinpoint people in need of food supplies. Snowdrifts were 15 feet deep in places. There was a rapid thaw followed by flooding a few days later. (*John Gent Collection*)

Circus, 1930. Lord George Sanger's Circus made regular visits to Croydon between the wars. In these more enlightened days performing animals are not welcomed but they were very popular in earlier times. (*Croydon Public Libraries*)

Glee Choir, 1930. Matthers' College of Music and Elocution was at 69 North End from about 1908 until at least 1939. Members of the Senior Glee Choir were immaculately turned out for their performance at the Large Public Hall in George Street on 2 April 1930. (*John Gent Collection*)

Ice cream van, *c*. 1935. The firm of C.H. Pacitti was based at 103 Windmill Road. Judging by the happy expressions on the faces of these customers their ice cream was very enjoyable. (*John Gent Collection*)

Carnival floats, c. 1938. This is probably part of one of the annual 'Streets of Adventure' carnivals that were popular from 1927 until 1939. Organised by Croydon District Traders they took place on a Wednesday (early closing day) afternoon, and raised funds for Croydon General Hospital. Croydon has had many local newspapers since the mid-nineteenth century, but the *Croydon Advertiser* has remained a most important part of the life of the town since 1869 and nearly always has a colourful float in present-day carnivals. (*John Gent Collection*)

The Crystal Palace, 1 December 1936. The disastrous fire that destroyed the Palace is still remembered by older people. Some ninety fire appliances and 380 firemen were unable to contain the blaze and this was the scene the following day. The Palace was erected on the Norwood heights in 1854, just over the Croydon border. It was a tremendous attraction for generations of local people for 88 years. The park can still be enjoyed but a famous landmark has gone forever, its site marked only by a television tower. (*John Gent Collection*)

Westow Hill, Upper Norwood, *c.* 1937. The removal of the Crystal Palace from Hyde park to the Norwood heights in 1854 was a great stimulus to residential development in the area. Upper Norwood grew into a high-class shopping centre. Until it was demolished in 1941, Brunel's great South Tower dominated this main shopping street. The boundary between the ancient parishes, and later boroughs, of Croydon and Lambeth runs along the centre of the road, hence the differing style of lamp-posts on either side! (*John Gent Collection*)

Floods at Purley, August 1937. Motor bus services into Croydon from the country and towns to the south were started by the East Surrey Traction Company in the early 1920s. When London Transport was formed in 1933 they were run by its Country Bus Department. Pleasure rides by bus into the country remained popular until the great increase in motoring during the 1960s. Here a front entrance STL-type bus on route 405 is making its way through the floods at Purley. Flooding here was a perennial problem because of the surrounding hills. A new drainage scheme has alleviated but not completely cured the problem. (*Croydon Public Libraries*)

Coombe Lodge, *c.* 1934. This house in Coombe Road is one of Croydon's older buildings, dating from the 1780s. It was the home of Sir Herbert Brown from about 1920 until his death during the war. Garden parties such as this were once a familiar part of the social scene in Croydon. The house was bought by Croydon Corporation and is now part of the Travel Lodge. The Council's Central Nurseries occupy some of the former grounds. (*Croydon Public Libraries*)

Coronation decorations, 1937. The decorations and illuminations for the Coronation of King George VI and Queen Elizabeth in 1937 attracted many visitors to the town. It was estimated that two million people came during the fortnight and that 33,000 cars were in or passed through the town on the last night of the celebrations. The arches in Katharine Street were also used as part of the decorations for the Jubilee of Incorporation of the Borough in 1933. (*Croydon Public Libraries*)

Purley Way Swimming Pool, *c.* 1936. The open-air pool opened in 1935 and could accommodate 1,200 people. It was very busy in good weather but its proximity to Croydon Airport led to its closure during the war. It reopened after the war but by 1973 repairs were urgent and it closed in 1975. The site is now a garden centre. (*John Gent Collection*)

Typhoid Inquiry, 1938. In 1937 a serious typhoid epidemic hit Croydon. Eventually the cause was found to be pollution in the Addington Well but not before 344 people had contracted the disease and 43 had died. In 1938 this Public Inquiry was held in the Council Chamber of the Town Hall. (*Croydon Public Libraries*)

Hospital Day, 1938. Before the days of the National Health Service, Croydon General Hospital relied on voluntary contributions and fees. Some of the nurses and doctors dressed up for Hospital Day to raise funds. (*John Gent Collection*)

Territorials, 1938. The ever-present threat of war during the late 1930s must have been in the minds of some of the onlookers when the 4th Queen's Territorials marched over Pitlake Bridge and along Lower Church Street after leaving the barracks on their way to training camp on 24 July 1938. A few of the houses in the left distance survive, but all the other buildings except for the gasholder were demolished in the 1970s. Roman Way and Jubilee Bridge now cross from left to right while Cairo New Road and a junction on the new tramway occupy the site of the shops on the right. (*Croydon Advertiser*)

Mitcham Road Barracks, 1939. The Croydon Territorials were mobilised on 24 August and some of their fond farewells were recorded by a *Croydon Advertiser* photographer. In the background is Croydon Power Station in Factory Lane. (*Croydon Advertiser*)

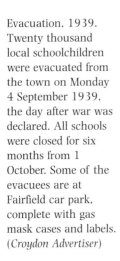

Evacuation, 1939. Twenty thousand local schoolchildren were evacuated from the town on Monday 4 September 1939, the day after war was declared. All schools were closed for six months from 1 October. Some of the evacuees are at Fairfield car park, complete with gas mask cases and labels. (*Croydon Advertiser*)

The Second World War

Mock gas attack, *c.* 1940. In the early days of the war there was great concern about the possibility of gas attack, and gas masks were issued to everyone; the advice given was to carry them at all times. A mock attack with tear gas in Katharine Street caught this woman unprepared and she is attempting to protect her baby by pulling its dress over its face. (*Croydon Advertiser*)

Ambulance and staff, 1940. As in the First World War, women had a very important role to play between 1940 and 1945 and this has undoubtedly had a marked effect on attitudes since. The staff of Brigstock Road Ambulance Station, part of the Civil Defence organisation, pose, with cats, in front of one of their ambulances in 1940. (*Croydon Public Libraries*)

Wardens' Post. The air raid wardens of Reporting Post No. H 39 pose for a photograph. This brick-built structure was on allotments in Regina Road, South Norwood. (*John Gent Collection*)

The Central Fire Station, *c.* 1940. Like most public buildings it was well protected by sandbags during the war. The Park Lane building was opened in 1906 and was replaced by the present one in Old Town in the 1960s. St George's House now stands on the site. (*Croydon Advertiser*)

Salvage collection, *c.* 1941. The Salvage Campaign started in November 1939 and eventually eight Salvage Shops opened in various parts of the borough, mostly manned by the WVS. Many people assisted in house-to-house collections. By the end of the war 37,885 tons of usable material had been collected in the town. (*Croydon Advertiser*)

First air raid, 1940. On the early evening of 15 August some German aircraft managed to avoid the coastal defences and bomb Croydon Airport before the air raid warning could be sounded. Houses and factories were badly damaged, sixty-two people were killed and thirty-seven were seriously injured. It was the first raid on the London area and a foretaste of what Croydon would experience over the next four years. Members of the Local Defence Volunteers (later known as the Home Guard) search for casualties later in the evening. (*Croydon Public Libraries*)

Injured people, 1940. Mr J. Coster, left, the manager of one of the factories affected by the Croydon Airport raid, and the man on the right with a bandaged head and hands, were injured in the attack on 15 August. (*Croydon Public Libraries*)

The Merchant Navy Comforts Fund, 1942. The fund was organised by the mayor, Alderman A.H. Harding. The 'ship' seen here, standing beside the lake in Wandle Park, appears to be a Corporation lorry in disguise. It was manned by members of the Heavy Rescue Service and later toured the town, raising, with other activities, 3,000 guineas (£3,150). (*Croydon Public Libraries*)

Shoppers sheltering, *c.* 1940. Customers and staff in a local department store take refuge in the basement during an air raid and wait for the 'all clear'. (*Croydon Advertiser*)

Christmas Party, 1940. People made the best of things during the war and this party was held in the shelter in the basement of Kitley's in North End in 1940. (*Croydon Advertiser*)

Croydon's Two Big Events

THIS SATURDAY at

KENNARDS

Official Opening

BY

HIS WORSHIP THE MAYOR

OF

CROYDON'S GREAT SALVAGE EXHIBITION

(PART OF SURREY COUNTY SALVAGE DRIVE)

3 p.m. SATURDAY

● THE GERMAN PARACHUTE How German housewives turned salvage into parachutes.	TURNING PAPER INTO SHELL CASES ● Special Working Exhibit by Munition Workers	● RUBBER SALVAGE PHOTO EXHIBITION
● BONES INTO MUNITIONS See what your bones can do.		● RAGS INTO ARMY EQUIPMENT
● Salvage Saves SHIPPING Special Exhibit.		● BOMBER WHEEL EXHIBIT

Exhibition Open Daily 10.30 to 5.30, July 18th to August 1st

ADMISSION FREE

AND

GREAT SOUTH of ENGLAND RABBIT SHOW

Official Opening

BY

His Grace THE DUKE OF NORFOLK

2.45 p.m. SATURDAY

● 4000 RABBIT ENTRIES	UTILITY SHOW THIS SATURDAY MONDAY & TUESDAY	● DISPLAY BY THE D.P.K.C.
● OVER 200 CLASSES		● 20 FAMOUS JUDGES
● £400 IN PRIZES	ANGORA SHOW THURSDAY JULY 23rd	● HOW TO KEEP RABBITS
● DAILY DEMON-STRATIONS	OPEN SHOW FRIDAY & SATURDAY JULY 24th and 25th	● RED CROSS AUCTION
● BUNNY VILLAGE		● SPECIAL PELTING DISPLAY

Entire Profits of this Show will go to the RED CROSS FUND

ADMISSION TO RABBIT SHOW 6d

KENNARDS LTD. — NORTH END — CROYDON

Kennard's advertisement, 1942. Many people kept rabbits and hens during the war, and 'Pig clubs' were organised to supplement the meagre meat rations of the time. Kennard's was one of the three large department stores in the town and was famous for arranging many bizarre and unusual attractions. Among these were some to help the war effort as shown by this advertisement from the *Croydon Times*. (*Croydon Times*)

Allders' department store, 1944. After a great deal of bombing during the Blitz, a relatively quiet period followed in 1942/3 and early 1944 although there were some air raids and some damage and destruction. On the night of 14 January 1944 there was no warning but a lone aircraft dropped two bombs on the town. One fell on the Davis theatre when an audience of some 1,500 people were present, but fortunately failed to explode. Even so seven people were killed and thirty-one injured. The other bomb fell on Allders' store. The lower floors were wrecked and severe roof and window damage was caused to the adjacent sixteenth-century Whitgift Hospital. (*Croydon Advertiser*)

Vincent Road, Coulsdon, 1944. The attack by flying bombs, or 'doodlebugs' as they were quickly called, started in June 1944. This incident at Vincent Road was one of fifty-seven in the Coulsdon and Purley Urban District Council area. (*Croydon Public Libraries*)

New Addington, 28 June 1944. This incident at King Henry's Drive caused serious damage to these and other houses on the edge of open country. (*Croydon Public Libraries*)

'Bombed out', 1944. A sad family group rendered homeless by a doodlebug in Croydon during the summer of 1944. Scenes such as this were common locally and are familiar to us today when we see pictures from other countries suffering the ravages of war. (*Croydon Advertiser*)

'Business As Usual', 1944. This was the wording on notices to be found outside bomb-damaged shops when people valiantly attempted to carry on as usual. If you were unable to eat your meals indoors because your home had been rendered uninhabitable you just had to make the best of it by eating out among the wreckage. Children often thought it rather an adventure but their parents were not quite so keen! (*Croydon Advertiser*)

Moffat Road, Thornton Heath. In a part of Croydon worse hit than others, Moffatt Road suffered severe damage from a doodlebug on the night of 4/5 July 1944. A horse-drawn cart is piled up with personal belongings, furniture is stacked on the pavement, and one couple take a few items away, precariously balanced on a pram, as they leave their shattered home. Scenes such as this were repeated day after day in the summer of 1944. (*Croydon Advertiser*)

Football crowd, *c.* 1940. The Crystal Palace Football Club is Croydon's professional team. Formed in 1905 they played at the Crystal Palace until the First World War, then at the Nest, Selhurst, former home of Croydon Common Football Club. They moved to their present ground at Selhurst Park for the 1924 season. Note that many of the men in the crowd are wearing hats, and most, but not all, of the spectators have their gas masks with them. (*John Gent Collection*)

Food production, *c.* 1943. Food rationing started in January 1940 and the government soon encouraged as many people as possible to grow vegetables. All available land was turned over to food production. Croydon Parks Department made their contribution, as demonstrated by this view at Coombe Lodge around 1943. (*Croydon Parks Department*)

The Home Guard stand down, 1944. The Home Guard was formally stood down at a parade on 26 November. Sir Malcolm Fraser, Lord Lieutenant of Surrey, takes the salute on the platform outside the Town Hall. The mayor, Councillor George Lewin, and the town clerk, Mr Ernest Taberner, are to the left. (*Croydon Public Libraries*)

Street party, 1945. Victory in Europe (VE) Day was celebrated with street parties such as this in Lansdowne Road, Purley. Thousands celebrated by singing and dancing in the streets, and there were numerous bonfires. The war ended with 814 people having been killed in air raids in what is now the Borough of Croydon. Many more were injured, and there was also terrible loss of life and injury in the armed forces. Over 2,600 properties were destroyed and most buildings in the town were damaged, some on several occasions. (*Croydon Public Libraries*)

Addington, 1948. This village was still a quiet and virtually unspoilt place in the summer of 1948. During the nineteenth century the Archbishops of Canterbury used nearby Addington Palace as a country retreat. Five of them are buried in the churchyard here. (*John Gent Collection*)

Selsdon, 1953. Some areas of open land on which building was proposed in the 1930s were not used because of the outbreak of hostilities. They remained into the 1950s but the urgent need for new houses saw building then take place. These fields at Selsdon disappeared under bricks and mortar soon after the photograph was taken. (*Croydon Public Libraries*)

The Late 1940s
and 1950s

Removing defences, *c.* 1946. Early in the war, large concrete blocks were placed in strategic positions to prevent aircraft landing or tanks passing in the event of invasion. Many were removed by council workmen after the war but some still remain. (*Croydon Public Libraries*)

Thornton Heath Pond, *c.* 1950. The view from the front seat of a no. 42 tram just before it turned into Brigstock Road reminds us that traffic was light after the war. Petrol was not available for pleasure motoring until 1953. The Granada cinema had opened in 1932 as the State and was renamed at the beginning of 1949. On the left by the trees Thornton Heath Pond was a reminder of more rural days, but sadly in 1953 this well-known landmark was filled in and now forms a traffic roundabout. (*John Gent Collection*)

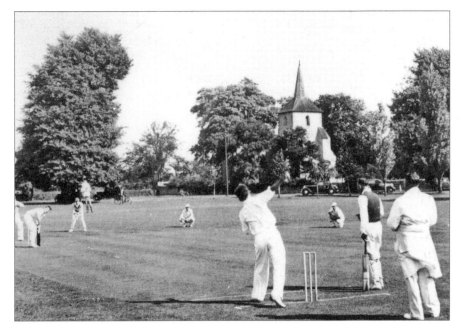

Cricket at Coulsdon, *c.* 1950. Here a game is in progress at Grange Park, near the church, which is one of the four ancient parish churches within the borough. Cricket has been a popular sport in Croydon for centuries and Addington has one of the oldest cricket clubs in the country. (*John Gent Collection*)

A group of children at Howard Junior School, *c.* 1950. (*John Gent Collection*)

International Festival Service, 1951. In 1938 Terence Driscoll founded the International Language Club and by 1939 it consisted of five houses in Addiscombe Grove. After the war the club had expanded to occupy some thirty-eight houses in the Park Hill area. They housed about 500 residents, many of them students and from a variety of races. By the 1960s redevelopment led to the club moving from the district. On 1 June 1951 the mayor and mayoress, Alderman and Mrs Stacey, attended an International Festival Service for students from the club at St Matthew's Church in George Street. (*Croydon Public Libraries*)

North End, *c.* 1949. Always a busy street, but now pedestrianised, most of the buildings on the right have changed little since this photograph was taken. The former Crown Hotel on the left ceased to be a hostelry early in the war and was demolished in the 1960s. The Civic Hall (formerly the North End Hall) was behind the public house. Tuesday

Lunchtime Concerts were started by the Corporation during the war, became a local institution, and continue to this day at the Fairfield Halls. A few doors further along was Wilson's shop and café. The aroma of roasting coffee drifting across the street was as familiar as the sound of the gongs of the passing tramcars. (*John Gent Collection*)

Prefabricated houses at New Addington, *c.* 1950. The building of a large private housing estate known as New Addington started in the mid-1930s. Work ceased on the outbreak of war, but the Corporation continued development from 1945 onwards. A large number of prefabricated houses such as these were built in various parts of the town to ease the urgent housing shortage. Eventually they were all replaced by permanent structures and New Addington is now a thriving community with a population of more than 20,000. (*Croydon Public Libraries*)

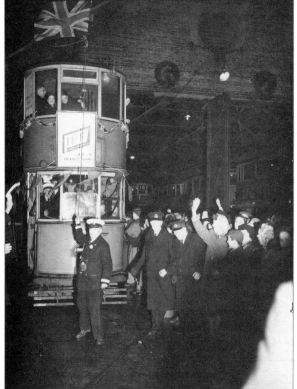

Last tram, 1951. The electric trams were withdrawn from Croydon's streets on the night of 7 April 1951. The last tram left Purley Depot for Thornton Heath Pond watched by large crowds, most of whom regretted the passing of a familiar form of transport. (*John Gent Collection*)

Battle of Britain Parade, 1953. The mayor, Alderman S.A. Maycock, took the salute in Church Street after a service in the Parish Church on 13 September. A permanent memorial to the battle has now been erected at Purley Way on the site of Croydon Airport. (*Croydon Public Libraries*)

East Croydon station goods yard, 1952. Horses were in regular use for many purposes until after the Second World War. The railways used horses for shunting wagons in the goods yard and for local delivery of parcels. Bert Andrews looked after the five horses here and retired when they were replaced by motor lorries. The horses are being loaded into horse-boxes on 9 February. It is to be hoped that he, and they, enjoyed a well-earned retirement. (*Croydon Public Library*)

Trolleybus, 1959. The trams on some local routes were replaced by trolleybuses between 1935 and 1937. They were later themselves replaced by diesel buses, the no. 654 route ran from Crystal Palace to Sutton in 1959, and the no. 630 route from Croydon to Harlesden in 1960. Here a 654 trolleybus is passing the Parish Church in February 1959. (*Croydon Public Libraries*)

The Davis' Theatre, *c.* 1958. This theatre in Croydon High Street opened in 1928. With over 3,500 seats it was the fourth largest cinema in Britain. Lavish stage productions also took place there, including appearances by the Covent Garden Opera Company and, in 1956, the Bolshoi Ballet, when queues for tickets stretched back half a mile, nearly to East Croydon station! The first performance by the Royal Philharmonic Orchestra under Sir Thomas Beecham was given here in 1946. Unfortunately, the general decline in cinema-going during the 1950s led to its closure and demolition in 1959. An office block, Davis House, now occupies the site. (*John Gent Collection*)

Park Street, 1959. It was then a quiet road with Victorian houses, mostly in use as offices. The crane visible at the end is a portent of things to come as the massive redevelopment schemes for the town centre got under way. The buildings on the right were all cleared away within a few years and the St George's Walk development now occupies the site. The street is now much wider and is one of the main bus stopping areas in the town centre. (*Croydon Public Libraries*)

Croydon Millenary, 1960. Croydon celebrated its millenary – a thousand years of recorded history – in 1960. The high spot of the celebrations was a visit by Her Majesty the Queen and the Duke of Edinburgh. The royal cars are turning out of Katharine Street on their way to the Technical College following a reception at the Town Hall. (*Chorley Handford*)

Millenary Pageant, 1960. As part of the celebrations a lavish pageant was staged in Lloyd Park with scenes from the town's history. This was also a large trade exhibition at the recently closed Croydon Airport site. (*Chorley Handford*)

The
1960s and 1970s

Air disaster, 1961. The whole country was shocked by a tragic air crash on a Norwegian mountainside near Stavanger on 11 August 1961. A party of thirty-four schoolboys from Lanfranc School, together with two teachers, was killed. Their bodies were recovered and brought back to lie in state in the school hall. The funeral service was held at Croydon Parish Church. It was conducted by the Vicar, Canon Warren Hunt, with a moving address by the Bishop, the Rt Revd John Hughes. Burial of all but two of the victims was in a mass grave at Mitcham Road Cemetery. The town was in mourning, traffic stopped and most of the shops closed. This floral tribute was being prepared in Surrey Street by the market traders. (*Croydon Advertiser*)

Steam in the snow, 1962. Most of the local railway lines had been electrified before the Second World War but the Oxted line retained steam until 1965. This evocative photograph by Stuart Pickford was taken from Barclay Road Bridge on a wintry morning, 2 January 1962. Park Hill Recreation Ground is on the left. (*Stuart Pickford*)

Construction of Fairfield Halls, 1961. The Corporation purchased the Fairfield site from the Southern Railway in the 1930s, but grandiose schemes for a new civic centre were thwarted by the war. The postwar plans for a new concert hall and theatre received a mixed reception from Croydonians and a town poll had to be held before the scheme was approved. Work on building the new complex was well in progress in 1961 and the early nineteenth-century cottages in Park Lane had yet to be demolished when this picture was taken. (*John Gent*)

Fairfield Halls opening, 1962. The opening of the Fairfield Halls on 2 November was a gala occasion graced by the presence of Her Majesty Queen Elizabeth the Queen Mother. Accompanied by the mayor, Councillor John Aston, she is shaking hands with Mr Malcolm Morris, Recorder of Croydon. Second from left is Sir James Marshall, Leader of the Council and Deputy Mayor, who was largely responsible for masterminding the redevelopment of the town in the 1960s. In the right background is Tom Pyper, the first general manager of Fairfield who laid the foundations for the great success of the undertaking in the early days. (*Croydon Advertiser*)

High Street, December 1962. The winter of 1962/3 will long be remembered for its severity. Deep snow lay on the ground for several months. A bulldozer is clearing snow in the High Street on 27 December. The National Provincial Bank (now the Spread Eagle public house) on the corner of Katharine Street is on the left. (*Croydon Advertiser*)

New offices, 1964. During most of the 1960s cranes and building work were part of everyday life in Croydon. This view across the Trinity School playing fields typifies the contrasting scenes in the town centre. The playing fields are now covered by the Whitgift Centre. (*Stuart Pickford*)

The Trinity School of John Whitgift. The school occupied this fine Victorian building from 1931 until it moved to new premises at Shirley Park in 1966. What a pity the tower at least could not have been incorporated into the Whitgift Shopping Centre now occupying the site. (*Stuart Pickford*)

Shirley Park Hotel, 1960. The hotel was housed in this lovely eighteenth-century building, surrounded by attractive grounds. It closed in 1961 having been bought by the Whitgift Foundation, which demolished it and built the new Trinity School here. (*Croydon Public Libraries*)

Croydon Summer Show, 1969. As part of the 'Holidays at Home' movement in the Second World War a summer flower, fruit and vegetable show was held at Ashburton Park. This continued for many years as the Croydon Summer Show with a variety of attractions until financial cutbacks led to its demise in the 1970s. The Guild of Social Service arranged this display in 1969. (*Ken Newbury*)

Public washhouse, 1963. Even by the mid-twentieth century many Croydon homes still had no bathrooms although home improvement schemes eventually rectified this. It was also rare for people to have washing machines, now generally regarded as a necessity. The Public Baths and Wash Houses at Windmill Road seen here in 1963 closed that year. (*Croydon Advertiser*)

Chair-mender, late 1960s. Street vendors and tradesmen were once common but are rarely seen today. This chair-mender was at work in a Croydon street in the late 1960s. (*Terry Cooper*)

Maltings, Church Road, 1970. Many familiar local buildings were demolished in the 1960s and '70s. Page and Overton's Brewery in Surrey Street closed in 1954 but these maltings survived until the 1970s only to be replaced by the ugly Post Office Switching Centre which dominates the area and really should have been sited elsewhere. (*Paul Sowan*)

Derby Road, 1966. Waterloo Place and Wellington Place (on the right) dated from about 1815. They may have had stables at the rear through the archways in association with the Derby Arms which was a popular venue for fox-hunting. These interesting houses were demolished as part of the Corporation's Handcroft Road housing redevelopment scheme in the 1960s. (*John Gent*)

Demolition of brewery buildings, 1964. Croydon had numerous breweries over the centuries. Nalder and Collyer's in the High Street ceased brewing in 1936 but the buildings remained in use for other purposes until the 1960s. In 1964 demolition was under way, including the two attractive Georgian houses alongside, one of which was for many years occupied by Dr Lambert Martin. The replacing Leon House has not done this part of the townscape any favours. (*Stuart Pickford*)

Park Lane, 1968. The road was being widened but St George's House (left) and the Fairfield Halls (right) were already familiar landmarks. (*Stuart Pickford*)

St Matthew's Church, 1972. The 1866 building in George Street formed a nice contrast with the new office blocks but was demolished in 1972 to be replaced by more offices. A replacement church was built at Park Hill to serve the new Wates estate there. (*Stuart Pickford*)

Cranes over Croydon – an appropriate title for this view of the Whitgift Centre under construction in August 1966. Similar scenes were common throughout the 1960s, part of the 1970s, and the 1980s. Recent construction work and planning proposals seem likely to mean more of the same in the twenty-first century! (*John Gent*)

The Whitgift Centre, *c.* 1970. The shopping centre was very innovative when it opened. One of the first major town centre shopping malls in the country, it proved very popular from the outset. By the 1990s it had become somewhat outdated and a major refurbishment scheme has brought it all under cover and transformed its appearance from that seen here. (*Croydon Advertiser*)

Horse Show, 1974. For several years in the 1970s horse shows, once a very familiar local event, were revived at Lloyd Park. Prizes are being presented here. (*John Gent*)

Heathfield, 1974. The early nineteenth-century house at Addington was for many years the home of Raymond Riesco. When he died in 1966 he bequeathed his fine collection of Oriental china to the town, together with his estate. The house is now being renovated and the beautiful gardens are open to the public. His china is displayed in the Riesco Gallery at the Clocktower. Part of the estate is farmland and is leased to a local farmer. Apart from an area devoted to pick-your-own produce, cattle are often to be seen grazing in the fields as in this view, barely two miles from the town centre. (*John Gent*)

Smallholdings at Selsdon, *c.* 1966. After the First World War land was provided for ex-servicemen to use as smallholdings. There were a number of these at Selsdon Vale, on not very productive land nicknamed 'Hungry Bottom'. Wates acquired the land for redevelopment in the 1960s and the area is now known as Forestdale. (*John Gent Collection*)

Carnival, 1977. Local celebrations for the Queen's Silver Jubilee included a carnival procession here passing through the High Street. Many street parties also took place. (*John Gent*)

Croydon, 1991. The town had earned its reputation as a mini-Manhattan by the end of the 1960s, but there was another lesser boom in office building during the 1980s. The dramatic skyline is shown by this aerial photograph with Taberner House (the council offices) on the extreme left, and the Fairfield Halls and Croydon College in the foreground. (*Chorley Handford*)

The End of the Century

Cherry Fair, 1990. The old tradition of holding a Cherry Fair in the town was revived for one year, and Church Street was closed for that purpose. Croydon Parish Church had to be rebuilt after a disastrous fire in 1867, but the tower dates from the fourteenth century. Six Archbishops of Canterbury are buried here. (*John Gent Collection*)

Croydon–Arnhem Link, 1983. After the Second World War Croydon developed a link with Arnhem in Holland, both towns having suffered badly in the war. The Arnhem Gallery in the Fairfield Halls is a permanent reminder of the association, and many exchange visits and events have been arranged over the years. This float was part of the Croydon Carnival procession. (*John Gent*)

Cooling towers, *c.* 1983. Croydon 'B' Power Station was commissioned after the Second World War but closed in the 1980s and, apart from its two chimneys, has been demolished. These six cooling towers were part of the industrial skyline for nearly 40 years until they too came down. (*Stuart Pickford*)

Charter Centenary, 1983. The town celebrated the Centenary of its 1883 incorporation as a borough. Her Majesty the Queen paid a visit and is in North End with the mayor, Councillor Margaret Campbell, welcomed by an enthusiastic crowd. (*Chorley Handford*)

Charter Centenary Exhibition, 1983. The Croydon Natural History and Scientific Society was formed as a microscopical club in 1870 and is the oldest voluntary organisation in the town. Its present-day interests range from ornithology, entomology and archaeology to geology and local history. The society organised an exhibition at Fairfield in 1983 to celebrate the Charter Centenary. The Exhibition Director, John Gent, is showing the mayor, Councillor Margaret Campbell, and the Chief Librarian, Tony Meakin, some of the publications produced by the society. The Town Crier, Dick Hill, looks on while Mr Campbell examines the local books. (*Chorley Handford*)

High Street, 1987. January that year brought particularly heavy snowfalls to the south-east. It snowed almost continually for five days and the railway tracks were completely buried so no trains ran for some time. This Leyland National bus had given up the ghost in Croydon High Street on 13 January and by the end of the week there was some 15 inches of snow on the level ground with much deeper drifts in places. Fortunately a thaw came within a few days but even so, provisions ran short in some places. (*Croydon Advertiser*)

The Great Storm, 1987. The same year was also notable for the great storm on 16 October. Croydon Borough lost around 75,000 trees that night, 100 roads were blocked and many buildings were damaged. Scenes such as this in Shirley next morning were common. (*Croydon Advertiser*)

Purley train crash, 1989. A serious train crash on Saturday 4 March left five people dead and eighty-eight needing hospital treatment. It occurred just north of Purley station and some of the coaches plunged down the high embankment into the back gardens of Glenn Avenue. Recovery of the wrecked carriages was difficult, as can be seen here a few days later. (*Croydon Advertiser*)

Folk Festival, 1983. For some years the Fairfield Folk Festival, hosted by Jim Lloyd, who lived in the area, was a popular annual event; this crowd outside Fairfield Halls is enjoying the occasion. (*John Gent*)

Selsdon Wood Country Show, 1996. The Nature Reserve at Selsdon covers about 200 acres and was saved from building by local and national efforts in the 1920s. For a number of years a Forestry and Country Show has been held there each August. The many rural atrractions bring large crowds for a couple of enjoyable days out as seen here. (*John Gent*)

Surrey Street, 1995. Archbishop Kilwardby, as Lord of the Manor, first obtained a charter for a market in Croydon in 1273. Surrey Street Market is regarded as the direct descendent of this and is usually thronged with shoppers. The triangle formed by High Street, Crown Hill and Surrey Street was probably once an open market place but by the seventeenth century permanent buildings occupied the site. By the 1890s the area had become very run down and a massive clearance scheme was undertaken so that nearly all the picturesque old buildings disappeared. (*Ken Woodhams*)

War Memorial, 1997. After some local controversy, additional wording was added to the war memorial in Katharine Street to commemorate the dead of the conflicts since the Second World War. The unveiling ceremony for the new inscription was held on 6 July. (*John Gent*)

Championship winners, 1994. The Crystal Palace Football Club has gone through a series of ups and downs over the years but there was a moment of deserved glory in 1994 when the team won the First Division Championship. The mayor, Councillor Pat Hecks, stands proudly on the Town Hall steps holding the cup. Members of the team stand behind, and Councillor Mary Walker, then Leader of the Opposition, has joined in the celebrations. (*Croydon Advertiser*)

Country Park opening, 1989. For some years South Norwood Sewage Farm, closed since 1967, was used by local residents for recreational purposes. In 1987 the Council decided to convert it into a Country Park. Mounting a horse is difficult at any time but Councillor Dudley Mead put on a determined expression as he helped Bernard Weatherill to do so in order to perform the opening ceremony. Now Lord Weatherill, Bernard was probably the best constituency MP the town has ever had. Even when his onerous duties as Speaker of the House of Commons demanded a great deal of time he could always find a slot for local functions and he continues to do so up to the present day. He was made a Freeman of Croydon in 1983. (*Croydon Advertiser*)

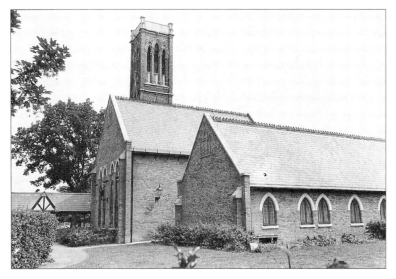

St James's Church, 1995. The second half of the twentieth century saw significant social changes. Patterns of churchgoing altered, partly due to general attitudes, and partly with the changed ethnic mix of the local population. St James's Church was built on Croydon Common in 1827 when the ancient parish began to be split up into smaller units to serve the rapidly growing town. By the 1980s it had become redundant and the building has been sympathetically modified by a housing association to form residential units. (*Ken Woodhams*)

Mosque, 1995. Just as some churches have become redundant, so the need has arisen for new buildings to meet the needs of other faiths. The mosque in London Road on the corner of Dunheved Road South was built in the 1980s as a centre for Islamic worship and study. (*Ken Woodhams*)

New library, 1993. At the beginning of the twentieth century the town had one of the best public library services in the country. By the second half of the century it was only adequate. The Council decided to revamp the Town Hall completely and add a new library building at the rear. Sir Peter (now Lord) Bowness, Leader of the Council (left), is with Councillor Eddy Arram, Chairman of the Libraries, Museums and Arts Committee shortly before the new library opened. (*Croydon Advertiser*)

Royal visit, February 1996. Her Majesty the Queen paid a formal visit to the Clocktower, as the new library and museum complex is known, while in the town for the 400th anniversary of the Whitgift Foundation. She is looking at the Lifetimes Exhibition accompanied by Chris Batt, Borough Librarian and Museums Officer, and Councillor Mary Walker, Leader of the Council. (*Picture Partnership*)

New library. This is on four floors, connected by escalators and a lift. The Lifetimes Exhibition (local history) is in the former court rooms. There is a 65-seat cinema named after the famous film producer and former local resident, David Lean. There is exhibition space, a café and bar, and the former Reference Library, the Braithwaite Hall, is the venue for concerts and is available for hire for special events. Apart from the excellent Lending Library with its Internet connections, there is a very good Local Studies Library and Archive Section. Croydonians are extremely fortunate to have such splendid facilities. (*Croydon Museums and Arts*)

Clocktower interior. The new building has been skilfully joined to the back of the old Town Hall (left) and an attractive circulating space provided between them. (*Croydon Museums and Arts*)

117

Queen's Gardens, 1995. The Town Hall Gardens were partly formed out of the disused railway cutting after the Central station closed in 1890 and the new Town Hall was built on the site. Throughout the century the gardens have been an important, restful and attractive feature of the town. In 1983 they were redesigned, and extended to mark the Centenary of the Borough Charter. Her Majesty Queen Elizabeth formally opened them as the renamed Queen's Gardens. They are usually much more crowded than this on a fine day. (*John Gent*)

The Whitgift Hospital, 1996. This Elizabethan building on the corner of George Street and North End has, since 1596, been familiar to generations of local people, and the final home for some of the elderly from the parishes of Croydon and Lambeth. The 400th anniversary of the Whitgift Foundation in 1996 was celebrated in style with a 'Tudor Week'. Councillor Robert Coatman enjoyed himself by representing the Archbishop in a Saturday morning 'Tudor' procession. (*John Gent*)

City status application, 1999. Croydon has for long been a city in all but name. As the sixth largest commercial centre in the country the town has made several applications for city status, so far unsuccessfully. The latest bid was on 1 September 1999 when a group of young people took the formal petition to the Home Office. Some of them are in Katharine Street just before departure. (*Picture Partnership*)

Tram track laying, 1999. The crowds that thronged the streets on the night of 7 April 1951 to bid farewell to Croydon's last tram little thought that they would see trams return one day. However, growing traffic problems and the need to improve east–west links across the town led to a new scheme. This links some little used and closed railway lines by street track across the town centre, with a completely new line out to New Addington. Work started in 1997 and here new track was being laid in Church Street in a scene reminiscent of similar work in other parts of the town nearly a century earlier. (*John Meredith*)

Crown Hill, March 2000. The first of the new trams ran on test through the town centre during the summer of 1999. The high fleet numbers continue from the highest numbered vehicle in the old London Transport fleet. Car no. 2543 is passing the Whitgift Hospital and about to descend Crown Hill. (*B.J. Cross*)

Addington Hills, March 2000. The tram routes run from Beckenham, Elmers End and New Addington into the town with one route continuing west to Wimbledon. There is a single-track one-way loop around the town centre. The route to New Addington is very hilly and runs through some of Croydon's most attractive countryside, as seen with this tram on test in the Addington Hills in March 2000. Public service started in May 2000. These two pictures demonstrate that despite 200 years of growth and development, Croydon is still a town of great contrasts. (*B.J. Cross*)